The
Economics
of Energy

The Pros and Cons of Hydropower

Ruth Bjorklund

Cavendish
Square

New York

Published in 2015 by Cavendish Square Publishing, LLC
243 5th Avenue, Suite 136, New York, NY 10016

Library of Congress Cataloging-in-Publication Data
Bjorklund, Ruth.
The pros and cons of hydropower / Ruth Bjorklund.
    pages cm — (The economics of energy)
Includes index.
ISBN 978-1-62712-930-5 (hardcover) ISBN 978-1-62712-932-9 (ebook)
1. Water-power—United States. 2. Hydroelectric power plants—United States. 3. Water resources development—United States. 4. Energy policy—United States. I. Title.

HD1694.A5.B53 2014
333.91'40973—dc23

                2013050644

Editorial Director: Dean Miller   Designer: Amy Greenan
Editor: Kristen Susienka   Production Manager: Jennifer Ryder-Talbot
Copy Editor: Cynthia Roby   Production Editor: David McNamara
Art Director: Jeffrey Talbot   Photo Researcher: J8 Media

The photographs in this book are used by permission and through the courtesy of: Cover by Tetra Images – Gary Weathers/Brand X Pictures/Getty Images; Science Source/Doe/Photo Researchers/Getty Images, 1; ©Mel Longhurst/age fotostock, 4; DEA/L. PEDICINI/De Agostini/Getty Images, 5; molinologe/File:Schiffmuehle02.jpg/Wikimedia Commons, 7; Saffron Blaze/File:3Falls Niagara.jpg/Wikimedia Commons, 8–9, 12, 16–17, 20–21, 23, 27, 34–35, 39, 46, 48–49, 52–53, 55, 58–59, 68–69, 73; Magnus Manske/File:John Smeaton.jpg/Wikimedia Commons, 9; ©Bill Bachmann/The Image Works, 11; Daderot/File:NMAH DC - IMG 8871.JPG/Wikimedia Commons, 13; Voith Siemens Hydro Power Generation/File:Sanxia Runner04 300.jpg/Wikimedia Commons, 14; Tennessee Valley Authority/File:Roosevelt signing TVA Act (1933).jpg/Wikimedia Commons, 15; Farwestern/Gregg M. Erickson/File:Grand Coulee Dam Panorama Smaller.jpg/Wikimedia Commons, 18–19; New York World-Telegram and the Sun staff photographer: Al Aumuller/File:Woody Guthrie NYWTS.jpg/Wikimedia Commons, 21; Mint Images - Frans Lanting/Getty Images, 22; David Walsh/B222-100-305/Reclamation Photograph Database, 24; U.S. Bureau of Reclamation/File:JohnKeysPGPGrandCoulee.jpg/Wikimedia Commons, 26; Jupiterimages/Stockbyte/Getty Images, 28; Business Wire/AP Images, 30; LostChain/File:BonnevilleSpillway.jpg/Wikimedia Commons, 32; Dtfman/File:Amateur Hydroelectricity.jpg/Wikimedia Commons, 35; ChinaFotoPress/Getty Images, 40; Ernst Haas/Getty Images, 43; Glade Walker/P549-100-2704/Reclamation Photograph Database, 44; Jeff J Mitchell/Getty Images, 49; DancingBear/File:Elwha Dam.jpg/Wikimedia Commons, 50–51; Ben Cody/File:Elwha dam remnants.JPG/Wikimedia Commons, 53; Ocean Power Technologies/NREL, 54; Jayme Thornton/Photodisc/Getty Images, 56; Bart Coenders/E+/Getty Images, 59; Jeff T. Green/Getty Images, 60; Cavendish Square, 62–63; Michael Westhoff/E+/Getty Images, 64–65; Mark Williamson/Science Faction/Getty Images, 67; Warren Gretz/NREL, 69; Oceanlinx/NREL, 70–71.

Printed in the United States of America

The Economics of Energy

Table of Contents

The basic concept of water wheel technology has stood the test of time.

Chapter 1

The Power of Water

The ancients believed in four basic elements: earth, wind, fire, and water. Early societies sought and found ways to harness the power of these elements. They learned that water was more than a vital necessity, and that it could also be an indispensable tool. Ancient Greeks fashioned wooden wheels with paddles and dropped them into waterfalls and rushing rivers. The paddles were connected to a shaft that turned a grinding wheel that milled grain into flour. Early Romans also built similar waterwheels. The design of the waterwheel was first described by a Roman engineer in the time of Augustus (31 BCE to 14 CE). He wrote that Romans generally used human labor for milling flour instead of waterwheels, but they did construct waterwheels throughout their empire to drive saws for cutting timber and stone.

Many early water wheels, such as this replica of a Roman water wheel, scooped water from canals for irrigation.

In China, during the Han dynasty (25–220 CE), the emperor instructed his engineers to create and build waterwheels for agriculture. Their design used buckets and heavy weights, called "pot wheels," that lifted water out of the river and into irrigation canals. By the Ming dynasty (1368–1644), the Chinese had developed waterwheels that turned axles and gears, thereby increasing waterpower.

Waterpower in European History

During the fourth century, Romans built a power plant in Arles, France, that used sixteen waterwheels to run an enormous flour mill. Soon after, when the East began trading with Europe along the 4,000-mile (6,437-kilometer) Silk Road trade route, components for making Chinese waterwheels arrived in Europe. In Medieval Europe (476–1066 CE), there was a notable increase in the number of waterwheel power plants. During this period, known also as the Dark Ages, Europeans suffered through numerous wars and serious plagues, vastly reducing the number of healthy workers able to physically operate flour mills. In the Domesday Book, one of the few written chronicles of the time, the uses of more than 5,500 waterwheel-powered mills in Europe are recorded.

As Europe entered the Middle Ages (1066–1500), inventors created new ways of using waterpower. They designed boat mills, which were flour mills powered by waterwheels that were built on boats and anchored under bridges. In later times, the mills would be built as permanent attachments to bridges. One of the first of several thirteenth-century London bridges built spanning the Thames River had thirteen arches, three of which were designed to house waterwheels. Two of the waterwheels powered corn mills and one was used to pump drinking water into the city. After that success, dozens of waterwheels were built under bridges throughout the city.

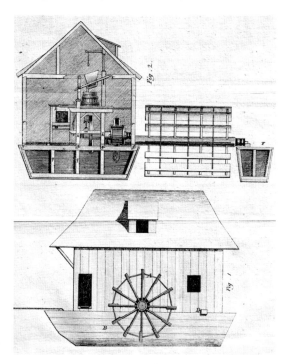

Shown here is a design for a boat mill. As far back as the third century CE, floating grain mills were constructed in European rivers.

Europeans also developed the first tidal mills. To power a tidal mill, they dug a small channel, joining it to a stream that flowed into the ocean. Waterwheels were then placed in the channel. The Europeans installed gates at the mouth of the stream, which opened inward as the tide came in. When the tide flowed out, the gates shut and the water dammed behind the gates was forced to flow out of the channel and through the waterwheels.

Waterpower was important to the mining industry in Europe. As the Middle Ages gave way to a more prosperous era, the population of Europe exploded. There were new battles to be fought, more money to be spent, and new items created for use in the home and in the fields. Demand grew for metals to make armor, weapons, farm tools, cooking pots, and coins. Water mills were used to run machines that crushed ore and extracted it from mine shafts, and powered giant bellows

A DEEPER DIVE

John Smeaton,"The Father of Civil Engineering"

Englishman John Smeaton (1724–1792) was the first person to call himself a civil engineer. He designed bridges, canals, lighthouses, and water mills. He invented a type of cement (known today as Portland cement) that could withstand being underwater. It is used today in dam and bridge construction. He was also the first to construct water mills using iron rather than wood. This was an improvement to both cost and efficiency because wood eroded so easily from the constant flow of water. In 1754, he proved through experimentation that overshot waterwheels were more efficient than undershot waterwheels. Water powers an overshot wheel by falling from above and using the force of its weight to push paddles, or blades, forward, while water powers an undershot wheel by flowing past the wheel's blades. In 1761, Smeaton devised

a powerful water engine for the Royal Gardens at Kew. This water engine turned a shaft called an Archimedes screw. A basic component of many machines (such as a fulcrum or blade), an Archimedes screw—or screw pump—transferred underground and low-lying bodies of water upward to create a lake and to irrigate the royal gardens. It was so advanced that it remained in use for 100 years before newer technology replaced it.

for ventilation. Waterpower was also used to separate ore from rock in a technique called "hushing."

The Rise of Contemporary Hydropower

In the mid-eighteenth century, a French **hydraulic** engineer wrote a book titled *Architecture Hydraulique* (Hydraulic Architecture). In it, he described several methods of using water to power machines. Most importantly, he emphasized that using a horizontal waterwheel was superior to the traditional vertical waterwheel. His work led to the development of water **turbines**, which are simple mechanically driven motors that use water to rotate blades on a shaft. Water turbines drove machines that not only milled grain and sawed timber but husked corn and rice, wove cloth, turned sugar cane into syrup, and made paper. In the mid-eighteenth century, Europe entered into the era of the Industrial Revolution. Factories manufactured more of the goods needed by society than ever before. Waterpower, or **hydropower**, was essential to operating the new machinery.

The Public Good

Early colonists brought waterwheel technology to the United States. Owners of millponds and landowners along creeks and rivers built waterwheels to power their mills. Those who did not build invited millers to lease their land and construct mills on their property. Laws in Maryland and Virginia encouraged the building of water mills for "the public good." In 1793, Samuel Slater built the first successful waterwheel-powered

Historic textile water mills can be found throughout New York state and New England.

textile mill in America, in Pawtucket, Rhode Island. Within twenty years there were more than 200 textile mills in New England, Pennsylvania, and New York. Water mills expanded to the American south to power machinery used in husking cotton and weaving fabric. In the nineteenth century, engineers developed water-powered turbine engines that, when connected to a **generator**, could produce electricity. No longer was it necessary for waterwheels to be directly attached to the machinery they powered.

Hydraulic Turbines and Their Creators

A water turbine engine, or hydraulic turbine, is defined as a rotary engine in which the kinetic energy of a moving fluid is converted into mechanical

A DEEPER DIVE

Thunder Alley

Water flows from the Great Lakes and thunders down a 170-foot (52-meter) precipice straddling the border between Canada and Niagara Falls, New York, spilling 750,000 gallons (2.8 million liters) every second. In 1759, Daniel Joncairs—the first recorded person to have harnessed a small portion of Niagara's power—built a small water mill near Niagara Falls to run his sawmill. In 1882, a small waterpower plant was connected to a generator that lit sixteen lights in the village of Niagara Falls, located slightly less than two miles away. In 1894, the Niagara Falls Power Company completed the construction of its first major **hydroelectric** plant, Powerhouse #1. Using the discoveries of famed inventors Nikola Tesla and George Westinghouse, it was the first hydroelectric plant to transmit long-distance power to neighboring cities and factories.

energy by causing a bladed rotor to rotate. There are two basic types of hydraulic turbines: impulse and reaction. An impulse turbine is a disk with buckets attached to a shaft. Water from a reservoir is fed into the turbine through a pipeline called a **penstock**. At the end of the penstock are nozzles that shoot a high-speed jet of water to rotate the buckets. One of the first and most efficient impulse turbines was the Pelton Wheel, named for its inventor, Lester Pelton (1829–1908).

The Pelton water wheel was first used in fast-running rivers near gold mining operations in California. It operated at 90 percent efficiency.

A close look at one of the Francis turbines installed in the Three Gorges Dam, China.

Pelton was a carpenter and millwright who worked in the California gold mines from about 1870 through the 1880s. Many of the mining machines used waterwheels, but traditional waterwheels did not work well in fast-running mountain streams. Pelton's new design operated at 90 percent efficiency and was a key to success in mining.

A reaction turbine is a circular plate with blades that rotate. A spiral casing surrounds its body. Water flows from a higher level down through the spiral casing. As it spills onto the blades at different angles, pressure is released causing the blades to react and turn the shaft. One of the most well-known reaction turbines was developed in 1848 by the chief water engineer for the textile mill town of Lowell, Massachusetts, James Francis. Called the "Francis turbine," it is a powerful and efficient water turbine that remains in use today by many hydroelectric plants, including the world's largest hydroelectric project: the Three Gorges Dam in China.

President Franklin Roosevelt signs the TVA Act, creating the Tennessee Valley Authority.

A New Deal

By the beginning of the twentieth century, nearly 40 percent of the nation's energy came from hydroelectricity. At the height of the Great Depression, President Franklin Roosevelt promised to fight back the "dark realities of the moment" by offering the nation what he called a "New Deal." Part of his plan created the Tennessee Valley Authority (TVA), an agency tasked with the goal to deliver electricity to rural America. At the time, 90 percent of city dwellers had electricity in their homes and businesses, but less than 10 percent of rural dwellers had access to electrical power. The TVA built hydroelectric power plants along the Tennessee River, one of the poorest regions of the country. Rural dwellers then joined city dwellers in having access to modern conveniences such as electric lights, radios, and refrigerators.

A DEEPER DIVE

United States Hydropower Timeline

1853 Niagara Falls Hydraulic Power & Manufacturing Company is chartered

1880 First industrial use of hydropower powers the Wolverine Chair Factory in Grand Rapids, Michigan

1882 Appleton, Wisconsin builds the first commercially used hydroelectric power plant on the Fox River

1887 First hydropower plant in the west opens in San Bernardino, California

1901 First Federal Water Power Act was enacted to issue licenses to construct, operate and maintain dams, reservoirs, and transmission lines

1906 Great Dam Act is put into commission

1907 Hydropower accounts for 15 percent of U.S. electrical production

1911 On the Salt River in Arizona, the Theodore Roosevelt Dam project is completed

1931 Construction begins on the Hoover Dam on the Colorado River

1933 Franklin Roosevelt signs the Tennessee Valley Authority Act

1937 Bonneville Dam, the first Federal dam, begins operation on the Columbia River; Bonneville Power Administration is established

1941–1945 Bureau of Reclamation hydroelectric dams increase power production to provide manufacturing support for World War II

2009 Hydroelectric power accounts for 7 to 9 percent of America's power supply

2012 The Three Gorges Dam, the world's largest hydropower project, operates at full capacity with 32 large turbine generators; the Federal Energy Regulatory Commission (FERC) issues first commercial license for tidal hydropower at the Roosevelt Island Tidal Energy (RITE) Project on New York City's East River

2013 President Barack Obama signs the Hydropower Regulatory Efficiency Act

The Grand Coulee Dam provides power generation for much of Washington State.

The Pros and Cons of Hydropower

In the early 1900s, a government agency, now known as the Federal Bureau of Reclamation, was created to oversee water resources in the west. Its main concern was allocating water for irrigation. However, in 1928, Congress authorized the building of a massive dam along the Colorado River that would power an enormous hydroelectric plant. This led to the construction of the Hoover Dam, which was dedicated by President Franklin Roosevelt in 1935. Its generators produced enough electricity for three states. During the 1930s and 1940s, the Bureau of Reclamation constructed other large hydroelectric plants such as the Grand Coulee Dam on the Columbia River in Washington State and the Shasta Dam on the Sacramento River in California. In the 1940s, hydroelectricity provided the west and the Pacific Northwest with 75 percent of its electrical needs. At the same time, hydroelectric power also provided one-third of the entire

A DEEPER DIVE

Darkness to Dawn

In May 1941, the government hired folk singer Woody Guthrie to write and perform songs praising the Bureau of Reclamation's hydroelectric projects, specifically the dams on the Columbia River. Critics criticized the dams, arguing that too much money was spent to produce energy in the wilderness. Guthrie wrote more than thirty songs extolling the virtues of electricity coming to the remote and rugged west. "Roll on, Columbia, your power is turning our darkness to dawn," he sang. A year later, as World War II broke out, the military's energy needs would surpass the entire nation's prior energy consumption. The lowest cost source of electricity to build airplanes, warships, tanks, and weapons was hydroelectric power. The ready supply of hydroelectricity in the west brought large defense industries such as steel and aluminum factories, oil refineries, and aircraft manufacturers. The Grand Coulee Dam supplied the energy for the Hanford Atomic Energy Reservation,

where the atom bomb that was dropped on Japan was developed. In 1948, Chief Justice of the Supreme Court Earl Warren declared: "Probably Hitler would have beaten us in atom bomb development if it had not been for the hydroelectric development of the Columbia."

nation's electricity needs. Today hydroelectricity supplies slightly less than one-tenth of the nation's electricity.

There are at least 8,200 hydroelectric power plants scattered worldwide serving more than 150 countries. The International Hydropower Association estimates that hydropower constitutes between 15 and 19 percent of all electricity produced in the world. The biggest producers of hydroelectricity are China, Brazil, Canada, and the United States.

The ITAIPU hydroelectric plant between Paraguay and Brazil delivers more power than ten nuclear power plants.

The Itaipu Dam, which straddles the border between Brazil and Paraguay, produces 90 billion **kilowatt** (90 **terawatt**) hours per year. Next in output is China's Sanxia Dam (also known as the Three Gorges Dam), producing 84 billion kWh (84 terawatt) per year.

In Canada, the combined hydroelectric output of all of the country's dams is nearly 89 billion kWh (88.9 terawatt) hours. The European countries of Sweden, France, Great Britain, and Norway actively pursue hydropower as a **renewable** energy source. Norway, with an output of 120 billion kilowatt (120 terawatt) hours of hydroelectricity each year, is the highest producer. This totals an impressive 99 percent of all the country's electricity consumption.

CRITICAL THINKING

- The uses of hydropower technologies were on the rise in the United States up until the middle of the twentieth century. Why do you think production stalled afterwards?

- Do you think the mega dams created in the west decreased interest in building more moderate-sized dams in the east and midwest regions of the United States? Why?

- Do you think too many hydropower dams were built, or too few?

- Do you think the United States should focus more or less on ocean energy versus enhancing its existing hydropower facilities?

These turbines at Grand Coulee Dam run the pumping plant that sends water to the other three powerhouses.

Chapter 2

Blue Water, Green Energy

Scientists estimate that there are 326 million trillion gallons of water on Earth. Water can be considered the most renewable of all resources because it exists in an unalterable and continuous cycle. Water evaporates from the ocean, moves through the air, rains and snows onto the land; pools into streams, lakes, rivers, wells, and aquifers; and ultimately flows back into the ocean. Converting water into energy is an ancient practice. Technology to make use of waterpower has evolved into one of the world's most inexpensive and renewable sources of energy. Hydropower provides 15 to 25 percent of the world's electricity needs.

How Does Hydropower Work?

The basic methods for producing hydropower have not changed from early times. Put simply, hydropower works when flowing water passes through a circular device that by turning produces energy as an output. Modern applications share the same principles. Where hydropower once produced mechanical energy, today it produces electrical energy. Moving water contains **kinetic energy**. As it passes through a water turbine, the

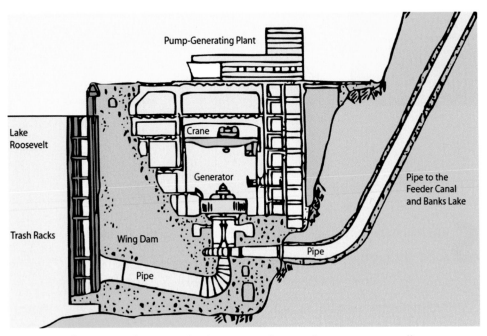

Diagram of a pumped storage hydropower plant in the Tennessee Valley Authority system.

turbine turns, thereby transferring the kinetic energy into mechanical energy. The water turbine is connected to an electric generator. The mechanical energy of the water turbine forces a rotor inside the generator to spin around a stationary rod. The spinning creates an electrical field around the rod and electrical energy is produced.

Types of Hydroelectric Plants

There are three types of freshwater hydroelectric power plants: storage, **run-of-the-river**, and **pumped storage**. Storage hydroelectric plants are the most common. They are usually built along large rivers. Concrete

A DEEPER DIVE

Measuring Electricity

Energy is the ability to perform work. Power is the rate at which energy is emitted. The basic unit of energy in the international system is the **joule**. The measurement of electrical power is calculated as a **watt**, which is the rate of using electrical energy in joules per second. One watt equals one joule per second. A watt is such a very small unit of measure that electrical power is usually measured in kilowatts (1,000 watts). A kilowatt hour (kWh) is the basic unit for measuring electricity use or output. A kilowatt hour is 1,000 watts of energy used over the course of one hour. For example, a 100-watt light bulb left on for 10 hours will result in its using 1,000 watts of electricity, or 1 kWh. The Grand Coulee Dam generates 21 billion kWh per year. Other large-scale units are the **megawatt (MW)**, which equals 1,000 kilowatts, and the terawatt, which equals one million megawatts or one billion kilowatts.

Chief Joseph Dam is a major run-of-the-river hydroelectric plant.

or earthen dams are constructed to hold back the rivers and form a lake, or reservoir. The hydroelectric plant is situated at the base of the dam. Towers on the dam take in water from the reservoir and feed it into a system of pipes known as the penstock. Water, controlled by a series of valves, moves through the penstocks. As demand for electricity fluctuates, the valves regulate the amount of water needed to speed or slow the water as it enters the turbines. The enormous penstock system created for the Hoover Dam used 45,000 tons of steel. The Hoover Dam was constructed using 5 million barrels of concrete and 582 miles (936 km) of steel reinforcing pipe. With stored water in the reservoir, hydropower plants can run consistently without concern for drought conditions. Dammed storage ensures that there is always a ready supply of water to move through the turbines.

Run-of-the-river hydroelectric plants do not use stored water. Instead, the river water is allowed to flow freely. It is diverted into canals or pipes and delivered to the turbines. Turbines are placed at a lower elevation in the river. After water flows through the turbines, it is released back into the river. Because the turbines operate without requiring a dam, land is not flooded so habitats are preserved and the river's natural flow is left undisturbed.

Pumped storage hydroelectricity plants are located between an upper and a lower reservoir. Water from the upper dam is released into underground pipes. It flows down through the turbines and out and into the lower reservoir. When electricity needs are low, water from the lower reservoir is pumped back up into the upper one. Often the water remains in the pipes underground and is circulated in a closed loop between upper and lower reservoirs.

Ocean energy research is leading to new devices that can operate off U.S. coastlines to produce electricity from wave power.

Ocean Energy

The use of hydropower in the oceans is a project in its early stages. For many states and countries, however, it is a promise of a new, renewable energy source. Oceans cover 70 percent of Earth's surface. Hydroelectricity is produced by extracting power from the kinetic energy in waves, tides, and currents; and from the thermal energy found in ocean temperatures. Hydropower plants using tidal power are specific to a certain type of geography, such as an **estuary** or narrow marine channel. However, the movement of the tides is both reliable and predictable. One method for capturing energy from tidal power is to build a type of dam called a **tidal barrage**. At the bottom of the barrage is a chute, beneath which are horizontal turbines. As the tide flows in, it enters the tidal basin, or estuary, and is contained by the barrage. When the tide ebbs, the chute opens allowing the higher elevation of the dammed tidewater to rush out and pass through the turbines.

Turbines that are installed in ocean current streams, such as the Gulf or Jet streams, can also produce hydropower. Other hydropower systems take advantage of wave power. There are three general types of wave power technologies: the Sea Snake, which moves on the surface of the waves; the Blow Hole, a structure near the shore that waves crash into; and the Archimedes Wave Swing, which is attached to the sea bottom and sways underneath the ocean's surface.

Hydroelectric systems can also extract thermal energy to make electricity. Within a closed cylinder, thermal hydroelectric power systems create energy by mixing cold water from the sea bottom with warm surface water. This mixture forms a vapor that in turn spins a turbine.

Efficiency

Unlike other renewable energy sources, such as solar and wind power, hydropower is constant. The sun can disappear behind cloud cover and the wind can diminish, but water continues to flow. One of the greatest challenges of effective renewable energy production is availability. The levels of demand for electricity do not necessarily coincide with the ability to produce energy at any given time. The electricity demands of households and businesses peak during the day, when wind or solar power may not be available. Solar and wind power rely on the ability to store power for later use. There is not yet adequate technology to store electricity long term. Hydropower, however, can meet the demand quickly. A hydroelectric plant can start up or shut down in minutes. When demand is high, it can increase output by speeding the passage of water through the turbines. When demand is low, water can be stored in reservoirs to be used later when needed.

The Bonneville Power Administration operates thirty-one federal dams in the Northwest. Above is the Bonneville Dam on the Columbia River.

Once a hydroelectric plant or project has been constructed, it requires little maintenance and can operate with energy self-sufficiency. Hydroelectric plants, as evidenced by the 80-plus-year-old Hoover and Grand Coulee dams, can be reliable sources of energy for long periods of time.

The United States Environmental Protection Agency (EPA) estimates that hydropower generates 9 percent of the total electrical supply for the entire nation. In the Pacific Northwest, where there is an abundant water supply, dams, including the country's largest, the Grand Coulee Dam, supply two-thirds of the region's energy needs. The United States' total hydroelectricity output can power 28 million households, which is equivalent to the usage of 500 million barrels of oil. A new hydropower plant planned in Alaska would generate 2.8 million megawatts of electricity and prevent about 1.3 million tons of carbon dioxide from being released into the atmosphere.

Hydropower is the most common form of renewable energy. It is renewable to the extent that the water used to power a turbine can be reused for other purposes beyond energy generation. This includes irrigation, a city water supply, flood prevention, or recreational activities (boating, fishing, or swimming).

Environmental Impact

Hydropower is one of the cleanest of all energy technologies. The EPA reports that hydroelectric energy burns no **fossil fuel**, produces no **greenhouse gases** or air or water pollution, and does not generate solid waste. According to the Hydro Research Foundation, hydropower is "America's largest source of clean electricity, accounting for 65.9 percent of all renewable energy generation in the United States." According to the American Rivers Association website: "Our nation is at a crossroads. We desperately need to reduce our dependence on fossil fuels and decrease the amount of carbon in the atmosphere. That means that we need to use less energy, and we need to get more of our energy from renewable sources. Thanks to modern environmental laws and values, hydropower's environmental performance has improved substantially.

A DEEPER DIVE

Micro Power

One type of alternative energy program on a small scale is a hydroelectric energy process known as micro-hydropower. The U.S. Department of Energy (DOE) says that **micro-hydropower** can be one of the most simple and consistent forms of renewable energy. A "micro-hydro" system is generally a privately or community-owned run-of-the-river type system with up to a 300 kW capacity. According to the DOE, a 10 kW system would be enough to power a home, a family farm, or small resort. For small communities and people living in rural areas, there are many advantages to constructing a micro-hydro system. It requires as little as the flow of two gallons of water per minute to take advantage of a micro-hydro system. Electricity can be transmitted up to a mile away. Depending on size, the initial cost of building a micro-hydro system ranges from $1,000 to $20,000. After the initial construction, operating costs are minimal. Throughout the world, aid organizations are developing micro-hydro

This micro-hydro system supplies electricity to a village in Cambodia.

systems in remote villages and impoverished regions, bringing electricity to countless communities from the Solomon Islands, located just northeast of Australia, to rural Alaska.

We need more clean energy, and yes, that means more hydropower."
The National Hydropower Association estimates that using energy from
hydropower sources rather than fossil fuels avoids 200 million metric tons
of carbon pollution (equal to the emissions of 38 million cars) each year in
the United States.

Waste Not

The Oak Ridge National Laboratory reports that there are 54,000 non-
powered U.S. dams in a state of good repair that have some potential
for installing renewable hydroelectric power. The report also states that
the top ten dam sites have a generating capacity of 8 gigawatts of clean,
reliable energy. Using existing dams for hydropower generation reduces
construction and start-up costs substantially. Many of the dams, the
report continues, can be converted with minimal impact to threatened
species, habitats, adjoining parks, or recreational areas. Environmental
groups such as the Sierra Club oppose developing dams for hydropower,
specifically older dams. Yet many of these older dams have been in
place for sixty years or more and have established new habitats of their
own. Destroying these dams would disrupt not only the wildlife that has
adapted to the surrounding environments but also the habitats that have
regenerated into a new normal. Properties owned by people who have
settled along the shores of these dammed lakes would lose value; parks
and recreation opportunities would be compromised. Also, many of these
older dams are on smaller rivers where endangered fish do not migrate.
Retrofitting these smaller dams would reduce energy costs for rural areas
and provide electricity to nearby communities.

The Federal Energy Regulatory Commission (FERC) has issued more than 250 preliminary hydropower permits since 2011. In 2012, the agency issued twenty-five new hydropower licenses, the most it has in a decade. The guidelines listed in The Nature Conservancy's document *Hydropower by Design* describe techniques in constructing new hydropower plants in locations where they will perform most efficiently while having the least impact on wildlife and habitats. States with the most potential for new or upgraded hydropower facilities are Illinois, Kentucky, Arkansas, Alabama, Louisiana, Pennsylvania, Texas, Missouri, Indiana, and Iowa.

Costs and Economic Benefits

Hydropower is a self-sustaining domestic energy supply that helps balance trade with oil-producing nations and helps secure energy independence. Hydroelectric power is not only sustainable, but it is the cheapest source of electrical power. When the cost of fossil fuels (oil, coal, or natural gas) increases, the cost of hydroelectricity production is not affected.

The cost of producing 1 kWh of energy using domestic coal-fired energy is just over two cents. Comparatively, the cost per kWh of hydroelectricity is closer to 0.6 cents.

In the book *Fueling Our Future*, author Robert Evans writes, "Although the capital costs of hydroelectric power plants are usually higher than those for thermal (oil, coal, and natural gas) power stations, hydroelectric plants normally have a much higher life expectancy, and with no fuel costs, provide a low-cost source of electricity." Hydropower consumes only 7 percent of the country's energy budget. With hydropower's proven efficiency and cost effectiveness, the DOE is funding research into more hydropower projects such as marine and hydrokinetic (MHK) energy production. The hydropower industry today employs more than 300,000 workers. By 2025, the department predicts that 1.4 million jobs will be created in the hydropower industry. In August 2013, President Obama, in keeping with his administration's goal of reducing carbon emissions and promoting renewable energy, signed two bills into law supporting new hydropower research, development, and construction. Both laws—the Hydropower Regulatory Efficiency Act and The Bureau of Reclamation Small Conduit Hydropower Development and Rural Jobs Act—received enthusiastic bipartisan support in Congress. According to Congresswoman Cathy McMorris Rodgers, a U.S. Representative for Washington State, "Hydropower is clean, reliable, renewable, and affordable. Unleashing American ingenuity to increase hydropower production will lower energy costs and help create thousands of jobs. The future of American energy independence depends on the development of an 'all-of-the-above' energy approach—and I'm proud that hydro is finally on its way to being part of it."

CRITICAL THINKING

- In what ways are each type of hydropower plant affected by river flow?

- If dams are demolished instead of being upgraded, what will be the replacement for the lost energy?

The weight of the water held back by the Three Gorges Dam is 42 billion tons (39 trillion kg).

Chapter 3

The Cost of Water

Waterpower may come from a renewable resource, but questions remain as to whether it is a sustainable renewable resource. Hydroelectricity carries high costs in many aspects: economic, social, and environmental. Critics of the development and use of hydropower ask if the cost and risks of hydro-generation truly benefit society as a whole.

Economic Risks

Hydroelectric power stations carry an enormous price tag. The Grand Coulee Dam, when built, cost the federal government $63 million. Translated into today's value, it would cost more than $1.1 billion. Construction began on the dam in 1934. It did not produce electricity until 1941. Even run-of-the-river hydropower plants that do not require the construction of a dam take a long time to produce power and incur immense start-up costs. Many years in the planning, a recent run-of-the-river hydropower project, the Meldahl Hydroelectric plant in Hamilton, Ohio, has taken more than eight years to develop and construct. Estimated building-related costs amount to $480 million.

It has been more than 40 years since a major "mega-dam" project has been approved and built in the United States. However, the Alaska Energy Authority has begun its application process for a massive new dam, reservoir, and hydroelectric plant called the "Susitna-Watana project." More than 3,000 scientific studies have been conducted since 1980. If the project is approved, as is likely, it will cost more than $5 billion and won't be operational until 2024. In China, the construction process of the world's largest dam, the Three Gorges Dam, began in 1992. Some experts estimate its cost to have been $88 billion. According to a report sponsored by the World Bank, the World Commission on Dams stated that more than $2 trillion has been spent constructing large dams since 1900.

Cost to Society

Dam projects have backed up 61 percent of the world's rivers. Once the dams are built, the reservoirs overtake the surrounding land, forests, farms, homes, and towns. People are forced to move or to adapt to a new way of making a living. The Norris Dam in eastern Tennessee displaced 18,000 people. The Three Gorges Dam made refugees out of 1.3 million people. According to the World Bank commission, dam construction has displaced more than 40 million people worldwide. Lake Mead, the reservoir formed by the Hoover Dam, has taken over approximately 247 square miles (640 sq. km). The reservoir behind the Aswan Dam in Egypt backs up the Nile River for 300 miles (480 km). Worldwide, many of the poor have been displaced by dams and have never benefited from the electricity, which is usually sold to the commercial and mining industries.

Work crews that constructed the Glen Canyon Dam lived in a temporary government camp.

During the initial construction of a major power plant, thousands of non-local workers move into the area. Many of the newcomers are employed for several years. It is expected that the construction of the Susitna-Watana hydropower plant in Alaska will bring in more than 1,000 new workers. Local communities strain to provide temporary housing and must expand other services, such as schools, roads, and public safety. Once a dam is completed, far fewer workers are needed. Those who remain hold specially trained positions. The Smithland Dam project hired 400 new workers, yet only nine will remain as permanent employees.

Teton Dam breaking loose.

Dam Failures

People living down river from a dam are at risk from flooding. "Dams provide tremendous benefits to society—from river navigation, flood damage reduction, and hydroelectric power to water supply, wildlife habitat, and recreation," says an engineer with the TVA. "But they also represent a public safety issue." Dam failures have many causes: eroding pipes, leaks and cracks in foundations and walls, erosion of the spillway, and earthquakes. In 1976, just one year after the 350-foot (109-m) Teton Dam in Idaho was completed, the dam failed. Flooding reached nearby towns, killing 14 people. The disaster caused nearly $1 billion in damages. The canyon site is in ruins to this day. The new Alaska Susitna dam project is in south-central Alaska, an area of active seismic activity. The proposed dam will be built only 40 miles (64 km) away from the site of a 2002 earthquake. Between 2005 and 2008, there were more than 130 dam failures in the United States.

Reservoirs can be their own worst enemy. Their very weight and size impacts the stability of the earth. Raising and lowering water levels can cause earthquake tremors in a phenomenon known as reservoir-induced seismicity. In 2008, eighty thousand people in China lost their lives when a dam failed due to an earthquake caused by the weight of the water in the reservoir. Scientists estimate that more than 100 earthquakes worldwide have been caused by dammed reservoirs.

Environmental Challenges

There are more than 80,000 dams in America, holding back the flow of an estimated 600,000 miles of river runs. The environmental organization American Rivers counts numerous ways that dams harm river ecosystems. Dams reduce water levels downstream and block the natural flow of plants and nutrients. Dams change water temperature, which affects species such as fish and waterfowl. This change also causes conditions that encourage new predators and invasive species to move into the area and destroy native species and habitats. Fish and other species can be left stranded without food and vulnerable to predators when water levels

A DEEPER DIVE

The River Dragon

Reservoirs and dams can be compromised by weather and geology, despite the best in weather-tracking technologies. New reservoirs must be built or older ones retrofitted according to standards that allow them to withstand monumental flood conditions. In August 1975, a massive typhoon pummeled Southern China with three days of torrential rain. Floodwaters crested over riverbanks and sixty-two dams burst, including the 380-foot (116-m) Banqiao dam. Combined, these dams spilled more than one billion cubic meters of water. The water roared downriver at speeds of 45 feet per second (14 m/s). Tens of thousands of people died in the raging water and 2.5 million acres of homes, towns, and farms were destroyed. In the aftermath of the disaster, called the "River Dragon" flood, thousands more were sickened by contaminated water and left homeless.

are lowered. Unnatural surges of raising and lowering water levels erode shorelines and alter lifecycles of fish and other wildlife.

Dams hold back more than water. They hold massive amounts of silt, sediment, sewage, polluted runoff, heavy metals, and other toxic debris. The more sludge the dam contains, the less water the reservoir can hold. Some of the sludge flows out and sinks to the river bottoms. When the flow of water is reduced, the sludge buries fish-spawning grounds. Dams also prevent gravel and downed trees from moving downstream, depriving fish and other wildlife of essential habitat landscapes.

Fish

Fish by far suffer the most impact from dams and reservoirs. Dependent on natural river flows, fish become confused when dams and turbines alter the flow and block access to all parts of the river. Reservoir waters, being still and deep, contain much less oxygen. When low-oxygen water flows downstream it kills fish. Native river fish do not survive well when trapped in reservoirs. Many dam projects provide fish ladders or bypasses around the dams and turbines. But only a small percentage of fish survive, specifically when they must swim upstream past multiple dams. Additionally, fish ladders and bypasses tire the fish. They then slow down, making it easier for predators to catch them. One method to protect fish from turbines involves loading them into trucks or barges and transporting them around turbines and dams. However, this method stresses the fish, increases their risk of disease, and upsets their navigational instincts.

A DEEPER DIVE

The Pacific Salmon

Anadromous fish, such as salmon, shad, river herring, striped bass, sturgeon, and smelt are severely affected by dams and turbines. They are born in freshwater but spend most of their lives in saltwater. However, the fish do return to freshwater to spawn. More than 55 percent of the Pacific salmon's spawning and fish-rearing habitat has been permanently blocked by dams. Pacific salmon spawn in the rivers of Alaska, Washington, British Columbia, Idaho, Oregon, and Northern California.

Salmon rely on a natural flow of water to deliver them downstream and to indicate when to return upstream. On their journey to the sea, younger salmon are battered against the concrete walls of dams and thrust into turbines spinning at 80 revolutions per minute. From the Snake River in Idaho, juvenile salmon must bypass eight dams. It takes them three months instead of one week. Juveniles such as these are forced

to navigate warm-water reservoirs, making them weaker and especially vulnerable to larger predators.

Historically, millions of salmon migrated into the Columbia River, providing a livelihood for countless communities. A healthy commercial salmon fishery has always been vital for the region's economy. Today, there are fourteen dams in the Columbia basin river system in Washington, Oregon, and Idaho. The river is 1,243 miles long (2,000 km) yet only 70 miles of it remain free flowing. Because of dams, at least fourteen salmon species are included in the United States Threatened and Endangered Species List.

Elwha Dam was built in 1913. Demolition began in 2012.

Tear the Dams Down

As early as 1900, people understood that hydropower plants damaged endangered fish populations and their habitats. In 1914, residents in northeastern Oregon dynamited a dam on the Wallowa River. It was the first dam to be removed in order to protect native wildlife and habitats. Since then, more than 600 dams in the United States have been taken down. The average age of dams in the United States is 52 years. Many of the dams were built in undeveloped agricultural areas. However, population in these areas has increased and more people are now in danger from high-hazard dams. Obsolete and underperforming dams are costly to remove. The Association of State Dam Safety Officials reports that it will cost more than $20 billion to repair high hazard dams. For dam operators, the decision to either spend money to repair and retrofit a dam or to tear it down is difficult. Yet allowing aging and obsolete dams to remain unchanged increases concerns over environmental quality, public safety, and sediment buildup. Dam removal, despite the cost, benefits society by reinstating natural river flow and habitats, restoring fish and wildlife, and providing recreational opportunities for citizens.

Deep Sea Power Drain

While many scientists and the government are involved with technologies surrounding ocean currents and wave energy, the cost of constructing these hydropower plants is prohibitive. The ocean can be a violent environment. In fact, once turbines or other means of capturing ocean power are installed, what happens to the power production is frequently

A DEEPER DIVE

Elwha River Dams

The Elwha River flowed freely for 45 miles (72 km) in what is now Olympic National Park in western Washington State. But in 1914, two hydroelectric dams were built to provide a lumber mill with power and they didn't have fish ladders. The salmon population then dwindled to the hundreds. By the end of the twentieth century, the nearby towns no longer used the power from the dams, yet the dams stood, blocking salmon and accumulating sediment. In 2011, the National Park Service and the Bureau of Reclamation began tearing down the dams at a cost of $351 million, the largest dam removal project to date. The Elwha dams could not be simply blown up. The release of the sediment behind the dams would block the flow of water and bury surrounding forests and beaches, swallowing wildlife and marine habitats. The Park Service explained the immensity of the project by saying that if they were to pile the sediment contained behind the dams onto

Elwha River Dam removal project was temporarily halted in 2012 to avoid excess sediment moving downstream.

a football field, the stack of debris would be five miles high. The undammed Elwha River will bring its salmon population up from 3,000 to 300,000, and will provide a habitat for bears, eagles, and the wildlife that once thrived along the river.

Ocean Power Technologies have installed wave power buoys off the coast of Hawaii that have been generating electricity since 2008.

out of the operator's control. Additionally, turbines in the sea would be a danger to marine life. Like wind power, waves may become calm and be unable to produce enough power to meet demands. The likeliest locations for ocean power plants are along coastlines. The nation's coastal areas are already dense with activity. Any significant ocean hydropower installation would impact coastlines and livelihoods for miles. Huge structures, such as tidal barrages, would overwhelm estuaries and marine channels, allowing no other uses, such as fishing and tourism.

Some deepwater systems are more efficient than shoreline systems. However the cost of bringing the power through underwater transmission lines, and the diminishment of power as it travels through those lines, removes most of the benefit.

CRITICAL THINKING

- Does it make sense to build a major dam in a remote region of the Alaskan wilderness? Why?

- Many of the country's largest dams are more than a half-century old. Do you think the costs of retrofitting or dismantling these dams should be built in to the cost of this type of energy?

- As you have read, impacts of dams and hydropower on fish, wildlife, and natural habitats can be devastating. Is it worth losing the energy output?

- Take into account the concerns over the failure and obsolescence of the aging of hydroelectric power plants in the country. Is spending money on new technologies in ocean energy the best option? Why?

Water bursting out of Jackson Lake Dam in Teton National Park, Wyoming.

Chapter 4

Hydropower, a Force of Nature

Proponents of hydropower believe that the resource offers an inexpensive, pollution-free, abundant and sustainable alternative to fossil fuels. As a renewable energy source, they say that it improves living standards and promotes greater energy independence. Detractors believe that hydropower installations are expensive to construct and retrofit. Many hydropower facilities are aging and are rapidly becoming inefficient, costly, and a risk to public safety.

There are valid concerns on both sides of the debate. Renewable energy and energy independence from fossil fuels is a realistic goal for the nation's and the world's energy demands. However, both sides must agree to balance costs and benefits.

Clean Waterpower

The American Rivers Organization acknowledges that despite the hydroelectric system's inherent concerns, hydropower is a part of our nation's "energy portfolio." However, making use of hydropower as a major component of renewable energy cannot come at the expense of damming new rivers or weakening environmental laws.

A DEEPER DIVE

Laws that Protect

In the 1930s, people began to realize that hydroelectric stations put stress on wildlife and native habitats. In March of 1934, Congress passed the Fish and Wildlife Coordination Act, which required the federal government to consider fish and other wildlife when proposing and building new dam projects. As dam projects were large and costly, it was usually only the federal government that could afford to build and run them. However, as private enterprise began developing more hydropower plants, regulations were needed to ensure that privately owned facilities adhered to similar standards. In 1948 the Federal Water Pollution Control Act was created. This was followed by several amendments, including the Water Quality Act of 1965. Later, in 1972, the Clean Water Act was signed into law to "restore and maintain the chemical, physical, and biological integrity of the

Dams up for renewal of their license undergo strict water quality tests. This man is gathering water samples.

nation's waters." The Act included standards that applied to public and private dam owners. In particular, the Clean Water Act requires that dam operators comply with strict water quality standards in a process called "Section 401 Water Quality Certification."

An Army Corps of Engineers inspector examines additions to the Ice Harbor Dam on the Snake River in Washington State.

The U.S. Environmental Protection Agency, the Federal Energy Regulatory Commission, the U.S. Army Corps of Engineers, and individual U.S. states oversee hydroelectric power generation. These agencies inspect and license hydropower facilities for safety and environmental compliance. Before any license is granted or renewed, hydropower facilities must be outfitted with the latest technologies that make the plants safer, more efficient, and cleaner.

The Army Corps of Engineers' National Inventory of Dams (NID) lists more than 87,000 dams, most built during the early to middle twentieth century. Most are privately owned and measure 25 feet (7.6 m) high or less. Martin Doyle, now professor of river science and policy at Duke University, wrote in *Science* magazine that many dams are "disintegrating, they are often not producing power, but their environmental effects are still there." Doyle added that in his home state of North Carolina more than 1,200 dams are considered "functionally obsolete." The NID reported in 2013 that there are 27,000 dams with significant to high hazard levels. Given that hydropower is here to stay, clean water advocates say that dam owners should install the latest technology so that the most power can be gained from the least amount of water. When dams cannot be retrofitted affordably, many dam owners find it more economically feasible to take them down. Since 2000, more than 500 dams have been taken down, many of them relics from the days of the Industrial Revolution. However, if dam owners can install effective mitigation strategies for fish, they could produce energy that is not only efficient but also environmentally sound.

Efficiency

Of all the dams in the United States, only about 2,500 are used to generate hydropower. The DOE produced a report estimating that the United States could increase its hydropower capacity by 15 percent if modern hydropower plants were to be installed in nearly 600 existing dams. Established in 1973, American Rivers is an environmental advocacy organization that protects wild rivers, restores damaged rivers, and participates in removing unsafe dams and improving operations of active hydropower dams. According to its website, the organization is in

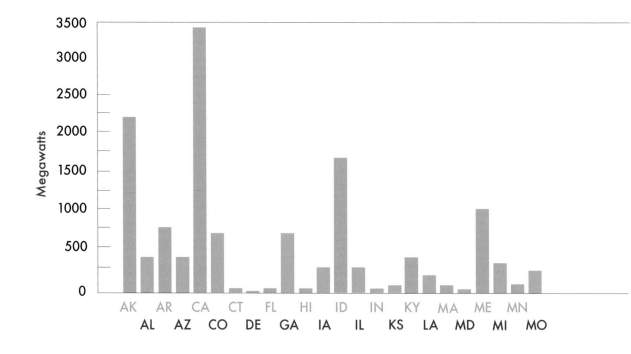

agreement with this strategy, stating: "Adding hydropower to dams in good repair that are still serving another useful purpose is appropriate if it can be done without further degrading the local environment that is already compromised by the existence of the dam."

Small is Beautiful?

With the 2013 passage of the Hydropower Regulatory Efficiency Act, Congress responded to the nation's needs for the renewable energy provided by hydropower. The Act allows a streamlining process for the development and licensing of small to medium hydropower plants that produce fewer than 40 megawatts.

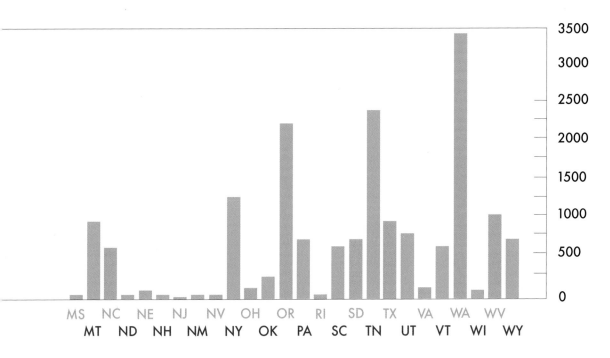

This Department of Energy graph shows the undeveloped hydropower potential for the fifty states.

The DOE will also be focusing more on run-of-the-river hydropower projects. According to the organization Green Energy Futures' website, run-of-river is the "kinder, gentler cousin of big hydro project." These are less costly to develop than dam projects and have less impact on the environment.

The greatest potential for a major increase in hydropower production lies in four river regions around the country: Alaska, the Mississippi River, the Ohio River, and the Pacific Northwest. The DOE intends to capture 120 terawatt hours of electricity per year from new turbine installations. The new legislation exempts licensing requirements for

Canadian and American hydroelectric power stations face each other along the Niagara River.

micro-hydro projects that operate under 10 megawatts of capacity. Many communities are developing another small type of run-of-the-river hydropower plant called streaming hydropower. Streaming hydropower relies on naturally falling water such as water flowing down in a mountain stream or contained in the pipes feeding a city's water supply. Las Vegas has installed streaming hydropower generators in its water supply line. Whenever pressure in the pipes build, instead of turning a valve to release the pressure, the water is diverted through the water turbines.

Smaller projects may or may not have a major impact on adding electricity to the power **grid**. Of concern to many environmentalists is the inconsistency of water flow in smaller rivers and creeks, which are heavily influenced by rainfall, snowmelt, and drought conditions. Furthermore, raising and lowering smaller dams profoundly affects the habitat. During the dry season, plants grow along the riverbanks. When the rivers and reservoirs rise, these plants are washed away. When reservoirs are lowered, underwater organic material is exposed, releasing greenhouse gases—carbon dioxide and methane—into the atmosphere. Methane is twenty-one times more toxic to the atmosphere than carbon dioxide produced by fossil fuel production. Environmentalists urge any development of small hydropower programs to take these concerns into account.

Hydropower development had been at a virtual standstill since the 1980s. Critics cited the environmental impact as "not being worth the energy output." Governments and communities, however, now believe that hydropower can be a sustainable solution to renewable energy pursuits. Many environmental groups are changing their attitude about the perceived damage to the environment, believing hydropower is a way to reduce greenhouse gases. The Nature Conservancy is working with the

U.S. Army Corps of Engineers and other private developers to produce sustainable hydropower. The Nature Conservancy has created a new task force called the "Low Impact Hydropower Institute," which is working with China and its Three Gorges Dam, and the state of Alaska's Susitna Dam project.

Going Forward

Several new technological advancements are on the horizon for making hydropower from rivers and oceans play a larger role in America's energy plan. The federal government has spent billions of dollars in improvements on its dams. Private operators are recognizing that spending money to upgrade their dams makes business sense. In order to comply with environmental requirements, such as protecting salmon as an endangered species, operators must spill water over the dams in order to simulate natural river flow and allow the juvenile salmon to migrate out to sea. While this benefits the fish, the hydroelectric output is diminished. The DOE reports that operators lose 8,500 MW per year and at a cost of $700,000 per project. Research by public and private companies has developed new fish-friendly turbines. Traditional turbines have five to eighteen spinning blades separated by gaps. Fish can be cut by the blades or trapped in the gaps. One new turbine has three large blades and no gaps. It spins slower, but because it is larger, it still provides highly efficient energy. The new turbine can convert 94 percent of hydro energy into electricity and provide a survival rate for fish of 98 percent.

In Pennsylvania, dam operators installed a fish elevator to lift migrating shad over the Safe Harbor Dam. On several rivers in the

The seven turbines operating at the Hoover Dam generate 4.2 billion kilowatt hours each year.

A DEEPER DIVE

Jewel of the Pacific

Two thousand miles (3,200 km) across the Pacific, the state of Hawaii has one of the highest energy costs in the nation. Given its location, the state relies more and more on renewable resources such as wind, solar, and ocean power. Hawaii's ocean power technologies are at the forefront of research and development. Ocean wave buoys installed in Kaneohe Bay in 2010 became the first ocean power plant in the country to transmit electricity to the main power grid. Hawaii is perfectly suited to ocean energy from ocean thermal sources as well. In an ocean thermal plant, large-diameter pipelines extend nearly 2,000 feet (610 m) deep into the sea. The installation is a massive heat exchanger. It pumps warm surface water, 75–83 degrees Fahrenheit (24–28 degrees C), into pipelines that pass around tubes of liquid ammonia. The warm seawater boils the ammonia into a vaporous gas. The rising and

Ocean energy companies are developing thermal plants in Hawaii to reduce the state's high energy costs.

expanding ammonia vapor turns an electric turbine. Cold seawater from closer to the ocean's floor is pumped through the pipes to cool the ammonia, so that cycle repeats. Scientists say that ten such plants could produce enough power for the entire island of Oahu, which is home to nearly one million people.

This wave power station is located close to the power grid for efficient power production and transmission.

midwest, companies are developing low-fall systems that do not require tall dams and fast-flowing streams to turn the turbines efficiently.

Waves of the Future

Ocean power—wave, tidal, current, and thermal—is making its way into the nation's energy plan. The federal government is granting millions of dollars to research the development of marine hydropower technologies. Pilot hydropower plants are being constructed on both coasts. The money is being used not only for development of efficient technologies but also for environmental impact studies on shorelines, offshore reefs, and marine life. The DOE calls ocean hydropower a "large, untapped resource" for renewable energy.

Hydroelectric power is capable of converting nearly 90 percent of its energy into electricity. Compared to fossil-fuel-burning plants that convert only 60 percent, hydropower is clearly the most efficient energy source. For its efficiency as well as its sustainability and reliability, hydropower is vital to the nation's energy needs. *The Wall Street Journal* reported, "Over the next two decades, hydro is expected to maintain its position as the largest source of renewable power and play a crucial role backing up intermittent generation from wind turbines and solar panels."

The nation is committed to developing new technologies in hydropower that promise to increase efficiency, lower costs, and take into account the importance of a clean and healthy environment. Earl Eiker, an engineer for the Army Corps of Engineers says, "Without water resources development, this country wouldn't be what it is today. We all like to know that we will have water when we turn on the taps, or lights when we flip the switch." To date, hydroelectricity represents the majority of renewable energy capacity and production across the country. It is flexible and reliable, allowing it to also serve as a backup resource for other renewable forms of energy generation such as wind and solar. According to the DOE, upgrading and expanding hydropower facilities is both the nation's challenge and opportunity.

Tara Moberg, a biologist formerly with the Bureau of Reclamation and a present member of the Nature Conservancy, is working on the new Susitna Dam in Alaska. She believes that the new hydroelectric project will be a showcase for an advanced, efficient, and environmentally sensitive source of efficient renewable energy. She stated, "I believe that renewable energy sources, like wind, solar, tidal, and hydropower, can be developed in a sustainable way ... What I see as one of our most valuable renewable resources is human ingenuity. These are solvable problems. We can meet renewable energy needs and minimize short- and long-term impacts if we have the motivation and flexibility for creative solutions."

CRITICAL THINKING

- What are your thoughts on whether large hydroelectric plants should be public or privately owned? Why?

- Should there be stronger environmental laws governing private dams?

- Should the government have more control of the activities of private hydropower operators?

- Which holds more economic promise: storage hydropower plants or run-of-the-river facilities? Which holds more promise environmentally?

- Should more dams be retrofitted for hydropower? Or should the money be spent on developing new technologies for run-of-the river turbines?

- Consider how you would spend your hydropower dollars. Would it be in tearing down unproductive and unsafe hydropower dams? Building newer, smaller, and more efficient power plants?

- Do you think that developing and repurposing existing dams for hydroelectric generation is the best compromise? Should there be a preference for small hydropower systems over large installations? Why?

Glossary

estuary: the area where a river widens as it meets the sea

fossil fuel: a fuel source made of decomposed prehistoric organic material such as oil, coal, and natural gas

generator: a machine that converts kinetic energy into electrical energy

greenhouse gas: a gas that traps the heat from the sun below Earth's atmosphere

grid: network of power transmission lines

hydraulic: a term to describe water or other fluids that move under pressure

hydroelectric: of, or relating to, production of electricity by waterpower

hydropower: mechanical or electrical power generated by moving or falling water

joule: a unit used to measure energy or work

kilowatt: a unit of power equal to 1,000 watts

kinetic energy: energy produced by movement

megawatt: one million watts

micro-hydropower: small-scale hydropower system

penstock: pipes leading from a reservoir to a turbine

pumped storage: a hydroelectric system with an upper and lower reservoir, where water is pumped from lower to upper levels during periods of low demand

renewable: an energy source that is never depleted or is able to regenerate

run-of-the-river: a hydropower system that uses moving river water without altering its flow

terawatt: one million megawatts

tidal barrage: a hydroelectric system using gates, chutes, and turbines to capture and release incoming and outgoing tides, situated in estuaries and narrow channels

turbine: simple mechanically driven motors that use water to rotate blades on a shaft

watt: a unit of electrical power equal to one joule per second

Find Out More

Books

Evans, Robert. *Fueling Our Future*. New York, NY:
    Cambridge University Press, 2007.

Friedman, Lauri S., ed. *Energy Alternatives*. Farmington Hills, MI:
    Greenhaven Press, 2011.

Haugen, David M. and Susan Musser, eds. *Renewable Energy*.
    Farmington Hills, MI: Greenhaven Press, 2012.

Langley, Andrew. *Bridging the Energy Gap*. Chicago, IL: Raintree, 2011.

Tabak, John. *Wind and Water*. New York, NY: Facts on File, 2009.

Websites

American Rivers
www.americanrivers.org

Learn about successful river clean ups and dam removal projects.
There is an interactive page showing how dams block and change rivers.

Read about how environmental concerns and the need for clean energy can work together.

Federal Energy Regulatory Commission (FERC)
www.ferc.gov

Learn about safety and development guidelines, inspections, licensing, and environmental mitigation of hydroelectric installations.

Low Impact Hydropower Institute
www.lowimpacthydro.org

Watch a video on the home page that showcases three hydropower projects involving U.S. rivers. These are great examples of hydropower success stories.

U.S. Army Corps of Engineers Dam Safety Program
www.usace.army.mil

Search "Dam Safety" on this website's home page to follow links to the Corps' activities, regulations, inspection strategies, and new safety guidelines.

U.S. Bureau of Reclamation
www.usbr.gov

This website provides a comprehensive history of the development of water containments in the western United States and present-day operations, including dam removal projects and fish mitigation strategies.

Index

About the Author

Ruth Bjorklund is a former librarian who has written more than thirty books on topics that include wildlife, science, and medicine. She lives on Bainbridge Island, near Seattle, Washington, where she enjoys hiking and the outdoors. Bjorklund has witnessed the advantages and disadvantages of hydropower firsthand. The dismantled Elwha Dam in Olympic National Park is near her home. This discovery sparked her exploration of the many hydropower plants in the Columbia Basin in Washington, Oregon, and Idaho, in particular, the Grand Coulee and Bonneville Dams, and the Ice Harbor Dam on the Snake River.